EVERY
LASH

PREVIOUS WINNERS OF THE VASSAR MILLER PRIZE
IN POETRY
Scott Cairns, Founding Editor
John Poch, Series Editor

Partial Eclipse by Tony Sanders
Selected by Richard Howard

Delirium by Barbara Hamby
Selected by Cynthia Macdonald

The Sublime by Jonathan Holden
Selected by Yusef Komunyakaa

American Crawl by Paul Allen
Selected by Sydney Lea

Soul Data by Mark Svenvold
Selected by Heather McHugh

Moving & St rage by Kathy Fagan
Selected by T. R. Hummer

A Protocol for Touch
  by Constance Merritt
Selected by Eleanor Wilner

The Perseids by Karen Holmberg
Selected by Sherod Santos

The Self as Constellation
  by Jeanine Hathaway
Selected by Madeline DeFrees

Bene-Dictions by Rush Rankin
Selected by Rosanna Warren

Losing and Finding by Karen Fiser
Selected by Lynne McMahon

The Black Beach by J. T. Barbarese
Selected by Andrew Hudgins

re-entry by Michael White
Selected by Paul Mariani

The Next Settlement
  by Michael Robins
Selected by Anne Winters

Mister Martini by Richard Carr
Selected by Naomi Shihab Nye

Ohio Violence by Alison Stine
Selected by Eric Pankey

Stray Home by Amy M. Clark
Selected by Beth Ann Fennelly

Circles Where the Head Should Be
  by Caki Wilkinson
Selected by J. D. McClatchy

Death of a Ventriloquist
  by Gibson Fay-LeBlanc
Selected by Lisa Russ Spaar

Club Icarus by Matt W. Miller
Selected by Major Jackson

In the Permanent Collection
  by Stefanie Wortman
Seleted by Chad Davidson

Other Psalms by Jordan Windholz
Selected by Averill Curdy

Booker's Point by Megan Grumbling
Selected by Morri Creech

Ornament by Anna Lena
  Phillips Bell
Selected by Geoffrey Brock

The Goat Songs by James Najarian
Selected by A. E. Stallings

Dream Kitchen by Owen McLeod
Selected by Rosanna Warren

Instructions for Seeing a Ghost
  by Steve Bellin-Oka
Selected by Peter Balakian

EVERY
LASH

LEIGH ANNE COUCH

Winner 2020 Vassar Miller Prize in Poetry

University of North Texas Press, Denton, Texas

10 9 8 7 6 5 4 3 2 1

Permissions:
University of North Texas Press
1155 Union Circle #311336
Denton, TX 76203-5017

The paper used in this book meets the minimum requirements of the American National Standard for Permanence of Paper for Printed Library Materials, z39.48.1984. Binding materials have been chosen for durability.

Library of Congress Cataloging-in-Publication Data is available from the Library of Congress.

ISBN: 978-1-57441-824-8

Every Lash is Number 28 in the Vassar Miller Poetry Prize Series

The electronic edition of this book was made possible by the support of the Vick Family Foundation.

Cover and text design by Rose Design

To Patch and Griff—
"the pair of black eternities
between which our little light intervenes"
because these are for Kevin too

CONTENTS

I.

II.

III.

I.

THE NEW MOON

I am warmed by the light you cannot see.
The night before I am new I am old;
and when new, I am invisible.
Do you want beauty? Try the empty
room at the center of a peach.
I used to think I had a mechanical heart.
It misfired, was fired upon, now it's hard
to tell the ripe from the rot: my heart
is sticky-sweet and fibrous but those
are just walls around the perfect
space. Calling it emptiness or absence is mean,
but it is unreachable.
I need to be silent to speak.
I need to putter and dawdle and sigh
to write what I know about the moon.
I need to be apart or I will break apart,
split the heart, dig a hole and climb inside
when nobody's looking. How much nothingness
is enough? I say, how much enough can you stand?
I say don't give up on failure. Answer rhetorical questions.
I can hear myself blink and I am a hero
who through unsubstantiated optimism
and slackness of spirit can get through anything.
This is a lie but one I can live with.
I am warmed by the light you cannot see.
The night before I am new I am old;
and when new, I am invisible.
I believe like the moon
each of us will sublime.

YOUTH

When soft was the sun and Neruda was the night
I was twenty-five and keeping the secret—

a forbidden pet I fed from the contents
of my chest, and in that windy closet

it curled, a pulse of glistening fur.
Windy was the weather at twenty-five

when I wanted my skin to taste
the world and never wanted to sleep.

I nursed the secret into unearned joy
when soft was the sun and Neruda was the night,

but the years kept coming, exacting a debt
I'll never repay. The more time you're given,

my young husband says, the more you have
to lose. The rich don't want to pay

taxes, and the middle-aged don't want to die.
In too deep we must press on, for death never fit

so well as it did at twenty-five when you and I
swam naked at dusk in the reservoir.

THE RAPTURE

Mouse, receive the hawk.
    Brain, seize your aneurysm.
        Lilac, accept blossoming as your Lord and Savior.

You were young and longed to sing yourself
    to death; you perched on ledges, asked God
        to plunder your heart, grew cold waiting for the wing-

beats in your ears. Today the gladiolas beckon,
    saying life is nothing less than lifelong
        resistance to dying, which is no art; and the mourning

dove in the deep woods tries to talk you into
    giving way to weariness, surrendering to
        how things are, in the sunshine, perhaps—

The dove in the deep woods moans,
    go on, you will not be left behind;
        buckling under has never felt so

ecstatic. Even his touch, the one you've loved
    the most in your resistance to this, is bothersome.
        You deliquesce and he must allow it.

Even as you slip beneath the still water
    death you think the unholiest thing.

Is that your heart slowing down or the great
    winged shadow passing over you?
        Being lifted up by your shoulders,

don't be afraid, this beast won't let you fall,
    having numbered your every lash and day.

IF THE EYE WERE AN ANIMAL

I said as I ran, *you are a beautiful boy*;
green words dipped and swerved like finches;
he ran alongside me the length of his pasture,
his hoofbeats circling my ribcage, unsettling the doves.
I said, *tired boy*, to the sleek calf's back
hidden in the high grass, and there a crow
unfolded to climb the sky. From its wings,
words fell around me, *blaze, blaze, blaze*.
I play the twin birches like a musical instrument:
missing is to *lost* as *go* is to *leave*.
To the spider bags or sacs of flies
woven like god's eyes in the trees' hips
I say, *batting, batting, the quintessence
of spring*. If the eye were an animal, sight would be its soul.

If the heart were a pond, woe to thirsty birds
in winter with nowhere to light
in the ice-sharpened woods and nothing to drink
from this frozen body, this frozen body that would
crack-spill open at a meager touch of sun:
this mirror of dead-seeming trees, *distill*.
Will fifty years be my alembic?
Circles get larger, multiply and intersect,
on the spring-fed pond. The eye is an animal
and leaves shimmy shimmy just before
the downpour. Is it possible to be loved
around loneliness? The cup inward flowing,
the pond can't resist the sluice, belly and stream;
errare and *eros* at once: a pond

meant to be a waterfall. The soul is water
in all its forms. You carry your daughter's grave

wherever you go: the comforter so rarely comforted.
Say the word *shed* aloud and see it
change color in the air, as blood, skin, light.
The rain ends, the sky grows fat with sun,
the sluice is full, and the pond wouldn't
think of running off. What follows is day
after imperturbable day of lavender composure.
What follows is the Gaelic word for lonely, *grave-still*,
and still . . . can you see, my animal,
where I am going with this? If the heart
were a body of water, mine more pond
than river or sea, love would be the levee.

AURICLE

A heart is the ear,
   canals and injudiciousness.
A heart is the oracle.
   We, aquariums for this one fish.
Love is not blood. Blood is air. Blood is water.
   Off kilter and compulsive, my heart.

The earth is a pendulum.
   The earth is the ball bearing inside.
The earth in the pit of the stomach drives
   a harder bargain than this one,
makes the future perfect before we can.
   We bob, we dangle, we adhere mostly.

   The armed heart holds on.
   My love is dirt and just the beginning.

A heart is the oracle,
   two deer on the airfield:
runway lights splash their hides steaming blue,
   their long necks swan-slide up and over.
Our hound comes home,
   matted with spider web and exhausted poison,

   a foreleg in his mouth.
   Your love is mutilation.

A heart is the oracle.
   My vigilance is primordial.
Your each blesséd day
   an image on a print.
I try to be the photographer
   who loves the dodge and burn.

But the earth doesn't move like clockwork;
   its twitch and pause might crush us all.

The earth in the jar's been shaken hard
    and set down on the counter.
Like my heart it jerks against wafer-thin glass.
    Bigger than the moon,

    Love is a sphere of solid iron,
    carried, floating, entombed.

When love fails, we found that the mind
    where you're made and kept
can be encapsulated,
    shelved in the cool still dark
to cure or sweeten,
    like canned peaches in the basement.

A heart is the ear,
    sternum to steel rail.
O Bartolommeo Eustachio, what do I do
    for this ringing in the chest
under the skin of every silence?
    Off kilter and concussive, your mind.

A heart is the ear,
    mine listens for seizure:
your mind's turn against us
    when love's a kind of misanthropy.
To the shrieking villagers I say, disappear,
    don't be more or less than polite, just don't look.

Love's the only vessel that looks on tempests
    and is never shaken—except
death, too, is a star for the wand'ring bark
    and when its gene finally settles in my heart—
when I am irresistible to dying—
    this smooth-muscled animal under my ribs,

    this ear, this oracle, this love, you
bear me over the edge of doom.

I AM NOT A MAN; I AM DYNAMITE

—Friedrich Nietzsche

Sometimes you are the single source,
the fist with all the flowers. Sometimes
you are the golden fish, a whisper-
revolution in this country of dust
stretching across the pond's dirty
bowl. Like a razor through silk
bedclothes, your fin breaks through
the tunnel of sky and one vain cloud.
Sometimes the hostage next door, you
are Sunday every day, and at night
a teenager in Auburn, Nebraska,
slamming an aluminum bat
to a goalpost until your head can't take it
to make something fucking happen.
Sometimes you are the single source,
the fist with all the flowers, a walking
iris, whose promise to die by late
afternoon makes you the word,
too much to bear. A syllable is
a latch, this word a door you shouldn't
have opened on a room, its very air
unstable with history. In the wrong
hands and right conditions such
a word will detonate, the way *ambrosia*
hides murder in its chest; to find
the *brute*, look for grieving; how
many souls packed themselves in
until Bethlehem beat them into *bedlam*?
You are the single source, the fist
with all the flowers—the bass, the razor,

10

the hostage, the boy, the bat, the ignition,
and yet we sleep on in this field of arms
where I am yours and you are mine.

FRAME

Branches reflected in the lake of mind
Nave, clerestory, and rose window of mind
Sears Roebuck house of mind
The sunny suburbs of mind
Sliding out through the masonry of mind
Blind fish of mind
Blue plum eyes of mind
In solitary of mind
Are you done with me yet of mind
The long-armed leaving of mind
Nostalgia is a pig in shit of mind

Ventriloquism of mind
Mind is the arbiter of mind
Rooks prey on the sparrows of mind
Poor lonely mind
Morning sun on the underside of mind
Emerging from the hoof-and-mouth slaughter of mind
Rising wild out of the red dust of mind
Hairless bone of mind
Florida blue-tailed skink of mind
Blasted out of the carport with daddy's shotgun of mind

Love is its own punishment of mind
A colored stone on the snow of mind
Cairns toppled by the deer of mind
Sea of mind
White-noise horizon of mind
The amniotic static of every day of mind
Field of mind
Field that clamors to the latch of mind
Great rolls of hay thundering over the edge of mind

HOUSE OF WIND

With nothing to carry, the wind is absence,
and whatever is carried becomes the wind—
snow, small rain, lilac air, men's voices like a grumble of bees.
The wind is everything or it is nothing.
When there's nothing to worry over I worry
there's nothing to hope for, as the hen who broods
in the monkey-grass under the mailbox: morning
after morning the hound roughly noses her out,
and morning after morning pretty eggs go rolling
down the street. The poor contrivances we live by,
simple enough in their construction: like two beams
moderately high driven deep into an expanse
of grass and buttercups. We cannot know where
they are in relation to the plain; to us the plain
looks infinite. This crude threshold between
within and beyond, before and after, through
and out, us and them—could it be our death-
defying escape? The train barrels through
the heart forever, but the bloody expenses
of springtime will never be fully restored.
In the garden I turn under soft heaps of down,
a thimbleful of bird, and cities of papery snails.
And though the crow stabbing at the doe's eye
is indelicate, her dismemberment is not without
ceremony: belly and loin to coyote,
haunches to wild dogs, flanks to fox,
soft innards to roughleg and red-tailed hawks,
and to pups just weaned go the ribcage,
hooves, and white flag—suture, rupture, ardor, raptor.
Morning clouds like silks wavering before
a listless sun. A rag of pop fluttering in
my head—"can you feel my heartbeat when I'm

next to you?"—my father—seen only in the
small hours drunk and dancing—returns
from the land of shame-not-forgotten. How
to keep him with me this time? To recall the scent
of lilacs in winter? We're born settlements
near the sea, bustling harbors of mysterious
traffic—some destined to be cities, others
pack their bags and travel far inland
to unsettled empty places where they build
their balustrades, their front door, back door,
their apertures. When the wind shakes
the trees, the *small rain down can rain*,
the barbed-wire birds drop the hay
in their mouths and commence their singing.

BIRD IN A BOAT

My goldfinch, house wren, lapwing, tin-whistle
swallow, apple-cheeked meadowlark, yellow-bellied
flicker, why won't you sing? My ginger bunting,

bloody tanager, leaky oriole, my Falstaffian jay,
why does your wing scrape the dust that way?
Your hiatus, grounded and mute, is taking root:

a loosestrife studding the bitter yards of mill-houses.
You'd want to know *hiatus* comes from the Latin,
to yawn. Always a drowsy bird, now you sleep

from dawn to dark. My nighthawk, vespertine,
short-eared delicately flammulated owl,
who cooks for you? who cooks for you?

What do you do, my battered canoe, on the black sea
night after night? Would it help to know
none of us are made true? A spec out of sync

in this mess up ahead, and the mind's a bird in a boat
searching for land: futile excursion in the dark,
where we lose our little canoe again and again.

KEEL

Who hasn't declared in the echo-chamber of herself,
I am the kind of person who falls in love easily,
drinks the smell of magnolias, and loves a good steak?
On the outside looking in, the mind as mentor
is always a few paces ahead of the sluggish self,
goading it to be identifiable. But if the dalai lama
is right, I no more cohere or inhere than a handful
of feathers dropped from a rocket. I am no more
than the remains of a thousand thousand days
at the bottom of a cup, my life. And all this suffering
is the lie of the self metastasizing, as lies do.
His Holiness tries not to mock but it does seem silly
to believe in a self set apart and waiting for me
to be born like a golden note waiting to be hummed.
He says peace be without you. These hands are nervous,
more tentacle than feather, and my mind won't be quieted
from its irritable tugging on the self *to be*. In the beginning
was an emptiness to be filled and the emptiness
was with me, and the emptiness was me.
In the Koran, Allah breathes life into mind,
heart, eyes, arms, hands, stomach, legs, feet,
and what does the new man say? *I am hungry.*
And Adam to Yahweh: *I am lonely.*
And in the first written English word, *keel*, I hear
a mighty ship groan and bang against its moorings,
and its captain saying, *I am small*; may this keel
cut through the dark waters of our monstrous ignorance,
splitting the world open like fruit.
From the high road my life is an old house,
with small windows on its jutting prow. It rides
one hill and one hill alone night and day.
Inside my own life I am a bird

in a cage dangling over space, listing
side to side in the wind, which is why
on most days I stay inside looking in.

MY DREAM OF YOU ISN'T OVER

Sono i silenzi in cui si vede
in ogni ombra umana che si allontana
qualche disturbata Divinità.

"THE LEMONS" BY EUGENIO MONTALE

From this high castle I hear a single bird
singing far below: I long to be small in the grass
and darkened by *il giorno più languisce*,
yet I can no more to you translate
my via Toscana at the turn of the century
than I can be translated years later from this tabletop
Tennessee into the folds of San Gimignano
where I climbed the towers alone, with Claire below
in a miasma of chianti and gnocchi from the night
before in Orvieto, and those fumes from the bus
as it whipped back and forth rising through the gorge
of hills—*bellissima*, no?—on either side.
We were young but afraid youth was ending.
We ranged through the land of the Etruscans
sleeping with men and women along the way.
Piero had a dog named Virgil, I remember.
We lay across the laps of coal-eyed boys in a cab
singing old Journey through the narrow streets
of Florence to deconsecrated dance clubs.
The next day we wanted the sea, and Italy
gave us a car! Was money exchanged?
Could they even see us? I didn't take a single picture.
I can write, *it was the season of asparagus and lemons*
though it may not have been. Saturated in the fields
green as blood between Siena, Pienza,
Montepulciano to Liguria, I never felt more
myself when certain I had disappeared.

Cypress becomes wind becomes breath and the traveler
is translated to *il punto mordo del mundo*—
the still point of the world, as Galassi
translates Montale, but I prefer Bell:
the blind spot of the world. For the poet disappears
through these fissures in the tower of Babel.
Finally worthless as a sparrow, I was a self
without precedent, inimitable and rare,
more clearly defined against that foreign
backdrop than I ever would be again.

LIFE IS A STATE OF SIEGE, A WAR
TO THE LAST WOMAN

—RANDALL JARRELL

Of all the gin joints in all the towns in all the world, I walk into his
    and right back out again to call my family: It's going to be awhile.

I need this drink with this man from two lives and three towns back,
    where spoons and forks tangled the yards.

His hands on my body I don't need but I might have hidden parts
    of my self in him, so let me flesh out my past

on those Revolutionary War streets where I rented rooms for nothing
    in an old boardinghouse, becoming the only tenant and caretaker

of rabbits and yellowjackets simmering in groundnests. I need this man,
    who is not my husband, to break in my heart its love of endings,

its longing for the dying engines of twilight when the dishes are clean,
    the laundry folded, the boys asleep. Not only childhoods get mislaid

in the terror of afternoons strangled into meaninglessness.
    What would that girl who ate bread and cheese under a bridge

on a dirty beach with strangers want with my life? How I miss her and
    the letter writer, lizard of many, dance-hall girl, lugger of sandstone,

stacker of wood, thrift queen, bookstore haunt, tinkerer of spaces—
    my dear companions dwindled to one, siloed and happy—

mother-wife. Home-soon, for now I long to be fluid, a tributary
    for all those selves rushing and laughing into our home. I know you all

would love me. This old boyfriend with eager eyes writes his number on a napkin
    and I take it. I take it to mean it's time to pack up, return

those rooms to vacancy, strip the sheets, bank the fire, turn the knob quietly
on my own sleeping house, and climb into bed with my youngest,

go blank with the warm damp smell of him. His words, thick and dreamclogged,
have you had enough of me, momma? burst my heart, that ripe fig.

THE HOUND ACCEPTS OUR NEGLECT

Forgive us, Fig, the cursory walks, the passionless
good dogs, our guilty faces too close to yours,
trying to get a kiss. Politely you turn,
and your straw-broom tail sweeps the floor
    with our fallacies.

Raising a paw to our shoulders, *There, there,*
you seem to say, *I have no words,*
so this should be simple: my body
is dog, my self you have named Fig, a name is expedient,
    A temporary stay,

like tagging a mosquito in a swarm. Ah, the self
is a swarm of dependent arisings. If there must
be I, I am the negative space in all
that commotion, not the forbidden sofa, not the dead frog—
    how sweet and delicious.

I am what the tick does not drink or bother.
I am the remains of your day after work, the boys,
and whatever else you do. Most of all
I am not your totem. I am something about to happen.
    I am never disappointed.

ON HOLLOW

Why are we here. Will love end.
Try hearing questions as declarations.
I need to tell you something,
the boy said, *what is hollow.*
Become a hollow thing before

the world. Expect the mind like a marble
to skitter and lurch and come to rest
in the center. Receive. Release. The clattering
frequencies. Let them tunnel through
you—crude whistle made of grass.

You are the lovers' copse in the woods,
the dark sky's starry cope.
You are the shine that comes from *shadow.*
You are the boy on his belly in the street
hanging over the culvert

stashed with secrets: a pair of cracked
glasses, a driver's license, a plastic foot.
Push up with your hands and run
to the other side of hollow, run
to catch the afterimage of you as you.

II.

EGGTOOTH

The fishhook in the beech tree, the X
of fallen pines across the path, the mirrors
in beads of rain, words are just outlines.

The bear in your doorway drawn
to the smell of frying bacon, language
is the wind through its coarse hair.

And language is the bacon. Which came first,
the chicken or the egg? It's hard to tell.
Words are albumen, chalazae, shell.

Something in the hatchling—not language or word—
but prehistoric urge wants to wreck
the nursery walls. Both weapon and tool,

the eggtooth she was born with before
she was born begins to stab membrane
by membrane out of the shell, like a wedge

in a sculptor's hand. When the first
spear of light stabs back,
the hatchling retreats, but the little she's known

is behind her, pushing her out into us.
With blind daring and that sharp eggtooth,
she pecks and shatters and carves

a new sun, a window, a doorway for leaving.
Language is the doorway made for leaving,
but mostly, it's the eggtooth.

EKE

Too many thesauruses my father left to me:
a diet of words and parables from the dictionary.
The mind is a closet with white walls primed
for its own projections, its St. Vitas Dance
of thoughts without words, words without thoughts.
The mind cuddling its old anecdotes like glass-eyed dolls
in the arms of ancient and addled women.
Had I more windows—I have one,
a playhouse door turned on its side—I could leave off
these rotten convolutions in my head. In the sure fidgeting
of the woods, the dead leaves' crunch and musky stew
into dirt, in the cinematic fits of light and wind
making shadows slide erotically across the porch,
through the glass doors, a dark dress dropped in my lap—
I could choose what to keep, to follow, to abandon.
Without a single word, I could write this, and this.

THE INDWELLING

The baby I thought I wanted
The baby that I got

The baby like a vacant motel room in Detroit
The baby gnaws at me with longing to be seen by you

The baby makes my heart a furnace
The baby makes my heart a stone

The baby swallows every word on the tip of my tongue
The baby brings strangers home to ridicule my singing

There's nothing diminutive about this baby
though it can hide for weeks
wailing and gnashing its gums at my neglect.

But when the baby plays the carillon
I walk into the cold street in my gown and bare feet—
that's how lovely the baby's playing is.

We all have our babies to bear:

to accept, to stand up to, to endure, to manage to tolerate,
to turn from and walk away, to take responsibility for,

to convey from apropos to overdue, from sadness to flight,
to mark us as their own, to carry.

And in return our babies bear fruit and grudges,
brunt and burden of the self
we scavenge and compose and therefore think

will hold us up. Our babies grin and bear it.
No one knows us like they do, having held us
in their little arms well before we were ever born.

HIBISCUS

A tonic, a tea, salmon dusk on the beach,
lambent light on skin like satin;
in the family of flowers back east: *marshmallow*
in Latin, for candy and medicine;
its Tokyo-tower stamen trembling in beads
of water shaken by a hummingbird
wing or tongue and, as a storm comes
to agitate an ocean, or a dragonfly
to discompose the standing water, a baby
screams, the day unloosens, hounds burst
through the wall of juniper and viburnum,
and somewhere surely a last word is spoken.

SEE ALSO: THE LAST WORD

Poor Adam, there was the debacle in the garden,
now the itchy clothes, and though he's told her again
and again it wasn't her fault (whispering low
we were set up), Eve in a corset of thorns
still mourns at the locked gates of Eden.
He'd begged that henchman Uriel for just a few
more days to finish. Who knew what might happen
to the unidentified. Would they disappear
like the mothering angels or the strange fruit that burst
on the palette with liquid color, music and sweetness
beyond compare? Beyond compare, because
Adam and Eve (unacknowledged herself) had not
finished the naming. Well, not really . . .

In all the hurly burly, hustle bustle
of eviction Adam slipped away for a bit
while Eve stalled in that still inadequately
theologized space where a presumably kind
God knows everything but lets humans
get away with far too much. In that space
Adam raced through the garden, within and without,
recklessly christening things, ideas, feelings,
this and that. It was offhanded,
there wasn't time (what a bother this *time*)
to touch, measure, get the best fit.
In this flurry of dubbing, our fluid language,
our wily tongue was unloosed.

                    Henceforth, praise
be the lexicographers! May they adjudicate
the unease of countless appellations (see also *appellate*).
          And praise be our beleaguered ante-
cedents! For by their cheek, their nerve, their gall,

we have this lingua viva, this argot, patois,
vernacular—language that word by word goes tromping
through the dictionary with muddy feet.
        O beautiful, mutable language that brings my soul
to its feet! Each word containing multitudes,
each syllable a hinge on new civilizations
and the human heart.

Those who say the Bible is the living word
then use it like a cudgel forget
how the word is riven and grafted, how *cudgel*
transfigures to *cuddle, coddle, caudle, cauldron,*
caul, and here we are, tenderly unhooking
Eve's bloody *corset.* Were it not
for Adam's effrontery (see also fifteen
synonyms for *impudence*) we'd never have tasted
                        that stranger fruit.

WHAT WE MIGHT THINK ABOUT
WHEN WE THINK ABOUT BLOW JOBS

The world is a cage for a woman, and inside it the woman is her own cage.

—RANDALL JARRELL
ON ELEANOR ROSS TAYLOR'S POETRY

Words are part of the problem, attribution
another, presumption another, and soon the problem

when observed from a distance fascinates with its roots,
branches, and veins: these veins hold blood.

A man and a woman walk into a room of mirrors
to talk it over: both expire, both walk out.

When a man slaughters me with words
I have a bad habit of fellating him then and there.

It's the only way I can think
to shut him up without causing a fuss.

A few minutes to feel less demeaned than
I do quietly nodding at his set pieces

fit for Narcissus and Echo; hypnotized by the droning
yet conditioned by years of such congress,

I still respond on cue, but deep inside the outer layer
of shine and nod I've gone feral, grabbing him

by the belt, unzipping, reaching in.
How did we come to this? What if he could see

my mind's grotesque flashes?
What if he could taste our sweet shame?

PRY

The stairs narrow as they rise, a quick embrace
of walls, my paterfamilias, before the flickering
door of my room and the pre-determined click.
I'd be dead in eight years were I Emily Dickinson,
with my thousand poems waiting not so nicely
in a trunk. And I'd know how to shelter and feed
that poetry were I Emily: my asceticism something fierce.
I would gaze out the window till my Soul
became watchable (Nature can take care of herself).
I would capitalize Soul, use dashes like bayonets,
train my meters to be unruly: wild and docile curling
into one another for their pleasure. I'd lower
warm bread on a pulley to the neighbor-girls below
just to be coy. No one could imagine my flights,
my fancies, the sounds of apple crunching against
my Emily teeth, without feeling irreverent.
I'd still have you. Your locked box I would be
and you would mean so little to me.

SLEIGHTS OF THE
CARTOGRAPHER'S HAND

Utterly lost in the land of long hours, I never strayed
but the trail strayed or rather the map was not true—
man's hand to nature misapplied or out and out lied
had made of the forest floor a shredded web and of me
a vagrant, spidering among the must and sluff of never-young
redwoods, their giant knees and heels bullying. Women
of myth turn to trees, stone, and salt, are put in their place;
the men who grieve are torn limb from limb, fall melting
from the sky in time-honored obliteration. I trusted the trail,
its gouge through the earth was relief for the map, which was
not true. It was not true and I was remade in amazement,
my past, a gibberish retranslated. It was not true
because it brooked no deviation, no creeks,
no bridges or other passes, and thus its assertion
into the wild was absurd and made me so.

WILD PIGS IN NORTH GEORGIA

Mr. Mullaney, I am a guest here
and cannot give you permission to kill
the pigs that upturn this yard every night
like puppies burying toys under the rug.
Whether it is with rifles or dogs,
in daytime or night, this is not my place
to say yes, which I suppose then is no.
You impressed me with your photos shot
by remote from a tree-mounted camera.
That is a big boar alright. And I sugared you
with questions about the meat, the spices thrown in
to the crockpot, making anything tender:
a nod to your broken mouth—a tarred
jumble, could be tobacco, could be worse.
But I cannot speak for the owner who lives in Atlanta.
I might have been frightened:
the screen-door between us, hook and eye
at the top, hook and eye down below;
you in formal camo, a three-piece suit,
to my gown and bare feet. You looked away
when you said, *I got permission from all*
the neighbors out to Dixon's farm, so don't
you worry if you hear the dogs tonight
or my truck—you and the gun were implied.
Something must have passed then from me
to you through the screen-door, hook and eye,
hook and eye, because you said *That sort of thing*
doesn't happen much around here. What sort
of thing, Mr. Mullaney? And when it does
happen, what do you know about it?
Mr. Mullaney, what have you done?

TEEN HUNGER

A story by way of introduction,
a story as proof you understand,
a story by which to connect, to stage a life, to misdirect—
this is none of those: I took what was offered
because finally it was offered. My longing
to be longed for was incorrigible. I didn't know
what I wanted because I didn't know—I guess
I wanted the bruises where they wouldn't show
made by a stranger who was the friend of the boy
on the other side of the bathroom door, the boy
waiting for what? The boy whose idea this was.
Just back from Paris, he'd made friends
with the Englishman and made money for wine
drawing caricatures on the street. So I can see
how the girl I wanted to be said *yes*,
though being asked is only part
of what I don't remember. The chain is still on,
and the door won't open all the way
on one of those nights where everyone
wanted so bad to feel good that meanness
ranged freely. I was there so the artist could fuck
the Englishman; the artist was there so the Englishman
could fuck a stranger; the Englishman was there
for his appetites. A bitemark around my nipple,
purplish fingerprints flourishing at my hipbones—
made me viable, I can tell you that. I want
to tell you more but the girl inside won't take the chain
off the door. She's afraid of what you won't see:
the humor in it all. This cosmopolitan proposition in practice
at a seamy Ramada in Atlanta, the rub-a-dub-dub
three of us in a tub, the sickly light and none of us
drunk enough. Or maybe she's afraid you'll see her

37

crying and mistake it for shame. I don't think
it was shame, more like despair, the hunger
still there, and nothing about her changed.

NEBRASKA

i.

This is a story of lecherous memory and the libertine—
memory, in fact, like trick photography, canned
peaches, the magician's coffin painted in dimensional
pitch but squirreled with rooms
like miscarriages, welts, and happy childhoods.

We come in to this world a Nebraska in winter.
Fact, like a beast on its back, the thing done,
pushes through limitless prairie, testing
its irrefutable self: mountains, sinkholes, fjords,
succulents, desert flame, aspen, and palmetto—

voilà! we're topographical and exotic when
the weather barges in, a Methuselan system,
a barometric mood hangs over a life for forty years—
painkiller unloosed from pain, feeling unloosed
from fact—it circulates through the heart,

an opiate flash, and how-much-it-hurt
razes the cell walls of what actually happened.
Don't forget our story of Nebraska in winter,
a beast on its back, the weather under our skin.

ii.

A hard bud like milkweed pushed up
inside her, she didn't ask for it, the bud
opened flap by flap, her girl-self,
an origami animal unfolding into
something beautiful behind almond eyes,
something omnivorous, impatient to arrive.

She was the looker and the one with a temper.
Those years my sister hated our *shit for family*:
her fury a needle-prick of laser light,
our home the brittle leaf (already talented
prey, I could track father's outrage and slip
away through cotton batting), I felt her bead

on my heart. My jaws tightened. The lash
began to stir. It happened to her and yet
the lecherous memory thrives in me—fed
and watered by shame so sweet to me then.
Is there a word for grinning and bearing it
when you're happy through and through?

I let my sister stomach the whole thing.
A pilled orange sofa in a claustrophobic den,
the wall leaning over them, scraping her knees
and forehead, my uncle pulling on her hands.
I told her I know, *I remember, it happened*, she told me,
and sitting on the floor outside the bathroom door

half closed, I told our mother. The door opened,
a Kabuki-doll tower, she *would take care of everything*.

iii. Symbiosis

She cut herself, tried to jump from a third-story
window between classes. The milkweed had cracked
long ago dispersing silk and golden scales.
She didn't ask for it. The meantime
grew a missile, a second bud on the same stem,
no less wondrous in its undertaking: slam open
slam open slam slam slam: encyclopedias, china,
metronome, knives, they flew from her hands.
An unappeasable goddess, she feasted on havoc.
If she wouldn't die, she would be heeded; her misery
turned medusa murderous, and our placid smiles
hardened like concrete as we rose higher and higher
on screaming pulleys and chains.
The fact is the memory never got out of our house.
The fact is my sister had always been an angry child.

iv.

Twenty years later over that feeble uncle,
she bends, his gray skin mottled blue, his neck
veins slack. We watch her brush his cheek
with hers, her children squirm in his lap.
It didn't happen to us, this thing done,
but its weather, how it curls around our spines.
This is a story of Nebraska in winter.
At Christmas dinner I told a friend about my only
opera: I was eighteen, I said, my father took me
in my first evening gown, we sat in the balcony,
his shaving crème smelled like pineapple.
After the story was finished: "That was me,
my mother said, "Your father was already dead."

OVERBITE, 1969

Go away, baby. I want to see the cars, the shoes,
the late-sixties Southern-spiffy clothes, the parents
and grandparents, the bully uncle, the aunt who must
be pregnant with Gary the way the camera lingers
on her stomach, but then your head with three teeth
(yes, count them) fills frame after frame.
Flap your little hand, baby, so we can move on
to the grandfather before he loses that slick grace
and most of his speech to a stroke one morning
while eating canned biscuits; on to the mod grandmother
in black polka dots who still worked at Penney's
before the stroke, after which she won't leave
the house on days she she can't
fasten her bra across the welts on her back.
Oh my god, it's Christmas! And the baby adores
her new green rocker. The other grandfather,
the nice one, loves to watch Pup-Pup lick the baby
from toe to forehead. The waves of laughter from this
happy happy baby are soundless. Go back to the teen
boys who look like runners at an ad agency
and never once ham it up for the camera.
The only sullen look caught on film
is from the bully uncle's son who grows up
to bully his mother. Most of all I want
to see the father and the mother and the father
with the mother—but someone has to hold the camera,
someone has to make the money, make
the dinner, take care of the baby, blow
off steam, see a man about a dog. The father
is so thin and with a lovely overbite
but the camera was his idea and his regard
for the baby of course, for old ladies caught

unaware, and for houses: Colonial, ranch,
Spanish, front doors, patios, even under-
construction, any house not his own,
he luxuriates in hypothetical lives.
The father is thin and, with a lovely overbite,
his smile, more like a grimace for the camera
or for the mother holding the camera for once.
The mother loves Peter Pan collars, cat-eye
glasses, and that baby, how the mother loves her,
and how the baby loves the mother's soft clean skin.
But the baby is just a baby acting the way
any baby would, so why this hitch in my throat
when the father reaches for her? I whisper
to the mute screen, to myself, *reach back,*
reach back, don't make him sad so soon.

HOME MOVIES

I do not reach back and no longer grieve.
This is where he lives now.
The nightly dreams where I bargain
him home have stopped. He's happier
in the sixties where the Lucky Strikes
never run out, his creased pants
hit the tops of his shoes just so,
and the women pivot and smile
when he comes for them
with a camera in his hand.

EROSIONAL

The memory of my father exceeded expectation.
After twenty-eight years has the little monk
finally turned its back on me? So many

peculiars the weather has licked and bitten away,
I can just make out the robe, his arms crossed
and tucked into the sleeves, a little irony

in rough statuary. The memory of my father exceeded
expectation. In a hundred years if no one
has carried it to shelter across her arms

like an unconscious child, his effigy will be
pulled down the hill, the way a trickster might
with slow care pull the rug out from under

a lecturer lost in discourse while his students
succumb to sleep: so fixed in conjecture he does
not feel the ground unresting beneath him

until he's let go, blundering down the hillside,
scattering finches in the grass; crickets and squirrels
might report on that day but how could I

remember forgetting him? His concrete cheek strikes
a rock, his head pops off, rolls hither
and thither, a tree falling far from its apple.

KILL ALL PARENTS

—YOU SAY THAT NOW

Children are meant to kill us—
we hope kindly, but dead.
Any lozenge of mercy would be
merely patronizing, a brief stay.
For twenty minutes our children abide
the deepest, most sustaining love
their blankness can receive. For twenty years
they crush our hearts. Here it is written,
their love for us—and I mean that helpless,
blinding, vertiginous, irresistible needle—
ends at their own perfection. Anything else
is blighted stone fruit at our feet.
I know my love will be made quaint,
then ridiculous, then obsolete, I know this
because I daughter a very good mother.

ANNIVERSARY

I saw a tall tree lean and lounging
in the crook of another. Both
were buoyant in green and spring thriving.
Both were straight and true and yet
one rested relieved in the arms of its equal,
and I thought, *succor*, a word I never say
in the company of others—unsure
of its meaning, quite sure what it sounds like.
From the Latin *succursus*, meaning
to run to help; a noun that must be helped
by a verb, as in "to give succor," as in
offering yourself to be loved, upheld.
To run to help: to leave to safeguard.
I'm leaving the woods to come home
to you and the bustling city we've made
in a thousand square feet of split level.
For too long I needed a father.
I am relieved instead I chose you.

III.

LIKE A GRASSFIRE

Nebraska's grasslands on fire like obedient children,
and I watch from the highway lullabyed in the murmuring

burn: a barely detectable tremor in the shoulder,
the winds finally bored were still. Not so bad,
not like California. There were trees yet.
These twilight fires seemed lazy, almost benign,
the smell of the land burning off was like kicked dirt
on campfires doused with dishwater.

You asked me to look at the valve sewn under
the soft ditch of your collarbone
where the radiation dripped in; you were sad,
scared, indignant. I was two states over
and started for home before the sun fell inside
the charred horizon, before darkness was complete,

when farther than the eye could see, the eye would see
how much the fires had claimed, crawling sideways
along the Missouri, gulping down anything
dead enough in the six-year drought. And I ran
from your bad luck like a stray ember,
from the news that all our names are stitched
                              on those fiery banners.

JELLYFISH GALLERY

A bloom, a swarm, a smack, a giant glass
of slick undulations through the water—
they look like brains! No, aliens, brother revises.
Neither boy ever has ever come screaming
from the surf, thrust his heel into cooler-slush,
or watched wide-eyed as daddy ate his cigarette
and plastered the hurt in wet tobacco to pull
out the sting. Before emerging into a slap
of light we turn left into the last chamber
of the aquarium: five hundred million years
and four walls of jellyfish—a slippery
illusion, a *mise en abyme* of mirrors in which
our eyes get tired trying to pry reflection
from depth and vice versa—a working definition
of *ennui*. In the midst of infinity I find

it's hard to breathe; my boys have years to go
before the age of recursion when every new day,
every new heartsting is swimming in déjà vu.
Of course we've been here before, dear
dour Ecclesiastes: the first few times
redoubling our efforts at change, at being
unprecedented, but our failure was resounding:
reductio ad absurdum. For we are the offspring
of the old cosmogonies but never spring far enough
to explode the chandelier, upend the tray
of Droste cocoa in the Dutch nurse's hands.
Syria was Rwanda when I was a child, then it was
Bosnia then Somalia. It's hard to breathe.

Past stars and satellites, ontologies and space
stations waltzing in orbit, past the earth,

planet and dirt, past humanity pocked
with infinity, past culture, past politics,
past my life, my body, I find the last
circle circulating, the tiniest jellyfish
in Tennessee: a coiled engine mixing
water and electricity like it's nothing, a heart
and only a heart, its neon blood flashing
in and out like an open sign.
It is a sign. A drop of green liqueur
feathers the clear water. Of all
the gin joints in all the towns in all
the world you walk into mine.

TO SOMEONE LIKE ME

Into the maple's big hands
the rain demurely falls
and no water finds ground.

The labial cut as the maple ages
gets deeper, ring and layer,
layer and ring, because someone

like me tied a sling for napping
in the late afternoon
because she could.

There once was a woman
who wouldn't release her facts,
resisting all quantification. Numbers,

dates diminished the power of production,
for she was her own writer, director, set designer,
and the lighting had to be just so.

The following is an experiment, but let this
be the control: I am not self-loathing.
Call me mother, wife, teacher, poet,

friend, daughter. Call me failure,
ear, eye, impassioned receiver,
connector of wires, tsk tsk, spark and light.

Then shuffle me like a deck of cards,
allow me to atone for our rapaciousness,
my people's loathsome final throes

and let me fold that at-one-ment
back in to my white self
to be embodied, elaborated.

For while someone like me
hopes to be remade, she's doubled
tripled, quadrupled instead.

HIVE MIND

We couldn't resist the enticements of the mind
as external organ. Night after night softening
into assent to the cyanotic glow of the screen.
O to be unsnapped from volition:

click, click, slight drag, click, pulled along
like children lashed together for a trip
to the swings, but some of the rooms we've seen
are too bright, too loud, too mean for the children.

The rooms are not the problem, but the house:
the collective keeps watch, reports back,
and buries us in a rubble of intimacies,
till the singular mind (mine) dims in its struggle

to know, be known, then unknow what it has seen.
Still sleek, still alert but, like an overfed dachshund,
unable to move very fast. The dog-thoughts
like bubbles in old seltzer break free of the glass,

prying loose, enjoying the smack of separation
and the zoomy rise that so smartly ends at meniscus,
or, in the case of the mind on internet,
the gelatinous scrim of consciousness.

AN ACT OF LEVITATION

This October evening the leaves hover
on still air like blossom, forms in mid-fall,
seconds (that's all), like photographs and not
dying (more if you will). One generation,
one year, one night, sharkgrass and dandelion
won't cover it anymore, and the dirt's refusal
of our refuse will reach us here in the woods
where metaphors ripen and fall, rot and re-
animate. And we carry on as if
the only illusion were this: nature, our trophy
wife, the obliging backdrop to a spring resurrection,
a June wedding, a messiah born on a cold
solstice, stars crowding in, twinkling
in wonder at what we have done. These days the sun
does not stand still. Levitation is just a play
of light. The sassafras leaves, pink and ochre, hold out
for nothing more than a memory of light: such rigors
of hope and compulsion, I understand, unlike
gravity, or what a person is supposed to do
with all this time, the history that will not die
in us from sheer neglect, the flush of shame
across my chest, when I think of you.
What's most real in a life is what goes on
unfulfilled, suspended mid-air: the child,
the poems . . . when all it would have taken was one
small impossible act, then another and another.
This October evening there's too much comfort
in knowing the end of the world isn't here yet.

LAPSE

We seem caught up in it, the lull of pure winter.
Crows in the distance, a chainsaw—life somewhere,
but not here. Not a single tremor in the shorn
saplings, not a squirrel or beetle shuffling the leaves.
The prey are too cold to eat: mice, rabbit, vole
knotted up under shuttered rhododendron.
Owls and wild dogs will need something soon
but now, nothing moves. Time arrested. Love
suspended. Were a buck to step in to this moment,
imagine the hysteria. But this desultory is to be
unraveled not broken: a single hawk swoops down
on a trembling pocket of fur scratching in the dirt
for seed. The ring slips down my cold finger,
a clattering on the floor, and finally you speak.

WANTING TO HOLD, WANTING TO FALL

Up-piled oranges holding their own
in sidewalk bins during rush-hour;
warm bowls, pots, dishes stacked
high and dripping to the floor;
a child's blocks in a child's hands;
a family for that matter; its foundation
exposed to the re-routed river,
the old house with sagging shoulders
knows what it wants—but only if wanting
opens its mouth (*just say the word
and I shall be yours*) to receive the mystery
of its collective will to hold or not,
to fall into the river or stand by.
The stories by which we live (the way
breathing out leads to breathing
in) are woven into the guy wires
that keep the snow on the rock face,
the shack on the mud embankment,
me with you. A summer day in the East Village,
through the bars of my fifth-floor window,
I see a pair of old hands behind the bars
of another high window open:
The hands, holding the bowl-
like body of a pigeon,
nudge the body through the bars into flight,
the hands gesture upward with the bird
what birds are meant to do.
But the weight remains a weight
and the hands, the bowl, the bird
withdraw into the dark room.
I have to think one day you and I will
give in to the pigeon's kind of falling.

PROMISE NEVER

We made plans in the dark, stitching up the seams
between falling in love & the rest of our lives,
making plans on our backs, real ones of consequence—
where we'd live, credit-card debt, were pinch collars humane?
You don't know everything about me—
like hearing a clock tick for the first time in a house
I'd inhabited for months; a swipe from a cat
I'd gotten too familiar with. *You don't know everything*
about me—a kind of instrument used more than once
with irritation, with sparkle—was I the cat & this
the dangling yarn?—then with despair at the end
of our idling: *you don't know everything about me.*
I'd read the Golden Book & did know
how to murmur soft & low, *we don't know*
everything about you, cajoling the beast, *we don't know*
everything about me, who might growl at my reach
but at my touch you groan & surrender & the second
I pull out the thorn are mine again. Night after night
this unknowing, year after year, this unknowing
would be the wisdom we'd use more than once
to work our way free of the obvious lines
that marionette the days of family & middle age.
Promise never to believe you can hold all of me & I
promise never to stop inquiring in the dark for you.

HOW TO MAKE A WOLF

The dog could smell love in our hands,
our eyes, our dozen words. The-things-
we-would-not-say would have to wait
until they no longer needed us.
Chickens roosted in the waiting.

When you kissed me in the bright kitchen.
When I slid down the wall with your voice
in the phone smashed to my chest.
Something stirred in the far dark, half alive
and making its way to our throats.

For its body we made a home:
parted curtains, deep-set eyes,
or parted lips about to speak,
about to think better of it.
The spaces were perfect around the-things-

we-would-not-say. The goats rarely
lifted their chins from thistle and thorn;
fear hunched in the wracked branches
and spiraling sighs—just the wind,
or the wind off the back of our creature circling in.

We will save each other from the world.
We will banish each other from the world.
In the loneliness of marriage will we grow shy
as two deer who do not recognize one another?
Will you miss me most when I'm in your arms?

For now we pass through the world in our home,
needing fewer and fewer words.
The goats blink their kaleidoscope eyes.
Our wolf is ready, teeth brilliant and long.
She softens her jaw to hold the master's hand.

LONELINESS FOR ANIMALS

Staring at the sloe-eyed cow, with dung on her backside, staring at me,
I think, what are you thinking?
She thinks, what are you looking at?
Which is speculation? From my side of the fence
I tear up a hank of grass—the pleasing sound cows make with their teeth—
and think, you'll come to me for this;
the sloe-eyed cow hangs her head lower
and thinks, why else would I?
An ineffable world within and without this one,
so close we can see the gray tail-hairs thinning
on the old squirrel, the ear twitch of the scentless fawn
waiting in the high grass, can hear the bodies of bees
knocking the glass below the eaves they're boring
into night and day—so close we could touch it.
But for them to touch us is what we long for,
to wander, curious and shy, onto our patios
like the young buck in the sandbox
sniffing the two-year-old's cornsilk hair;
the mother said, *it keeps coming back, its fur smells like sawdust.*
We know this won't end well.
It was not a necessary kindness
for the man to scoop up the mewling bundle
and keep the hairless squirrel hidden in his jacket pocket
while he fed it formula for weeks from a dropper at work.
It sat on the man's shoulders while he shaved,
cried every time he left the room.
He had been lonely for just this
kind of belonging: the lakelike gaze of an animal
reassures—like the self we suspect inside the self.
But theirs is not a world within ours
and the wild never wants us for long enough.

FLYING SQUIRREL

The lady down the way, whose woods these are,
calls them boomers. I call them solo slam-dancers
on cold nights checking ID's at my attic door.
Once named, the gentleman squirrel could be talked to
over coffee and toast each morning
in our adjoining chambers. But the beast
kept breaking character with erratic frenzy.
Could this part bird, part bat, part arboreal rat
slip a tiny claw through the hatch, popping open
the eyehook? Warmed by my breath, would he curl
tail to forehead on the pillow, generously slipping
nuts and seed into my open mouth while I slept?
Would a frightened boomer prick out my eyes;
with needle teeth, would he bite at my heels?

I know what a frightened renter of cabins in the woods
would do: allow the handyman his pearls of poison
and too late wonder where it might end:
Midflight, unwell all morning, the shadow-tail would drop
into a leafy grave where he's dinner and a warm bed
for midges and maggots; the steam of his waste
rising like a kite to a hawk or a fox, and, unless her pups
are waiting for their milk, the fox is where the poison
might end. But the renter would be wrong again.
For the creature, being like her in ways she can't understand,
being sick and alone, does not feel like a swinger
of birches and crawls back home, a soft thup,
thup, thup in his quarters above.

SUMMER ENDS IN VIRGINIA

Cow

Dusky multitudes wander the grassless fields
along I-40 nine-hundred miles from here.
Dazed in the heat, on radioactive feed,
they go from birth to enormous in a few months' time.
As far as the eye can see, heads
dip and rise, dip and rise, dip and rise.
You will not make the cow a metaphor.
The impassive anvil is enough.
Cows bawling and pushed into metal stalls
by burly men at their hindquarters is enough:
the hammer slammed, her flat head,
the whites of her eyes, then red.

Spider

to the poet with goddamn spiderweb in her eyelashes,
arm-hair, and teeth, because she was smiling
to herself opening the iron gate—a secret
in the boxwoods—onto the pond, marbled green
with algae, to look for goldfish:

Your bulldozers haul the sun up every morning.
Your touch, the baptism of concrete.
You fill the spaces between what you build
with speed and bodies. Leave us
some air to work with.

Cow

we were something slow happening inside the cold brain of a
cow . . . the remote, massive unvindictive indifference of God
all-mighty or fate or me
                                              —ROBERT PENN WARREN

You will not write about the cow.
You will not write, Her thick-slippery
tongue, whitish pink, slaps at her buggy
sides and sticky udder. You won't put the cow
on a pedestal, an inconvenience in her bowing
to sweet clover, up and down, up and down.

In her solid gaze, best called bovine,
blackflies swim in peripheral liquid,
and there you are, barely in focus, there
you go again—a soft shifty blur.
She says, here it's all the same.
She says, our many stomachs are unperturbed.

She must, like us, haul herself
through space and time, one field
to another, but you've never seen it.
A low cloud passes over onion,
goldenrod, fool's corn, carrot grass:
her shadow through nighttime

to the next morning's tableau:
constant hunger, patient fulfillment,
milling about with the others, chewing.

Pigeon

Description is not the point.
After dinner we watched the pigeons fly.
Too top-heavy and round to surf the licks of wind
brought in by another hurricane nine-hundred miles away,
they dive, weave, dip, weave, dive.
A banner unloosed, the flock
circles closer and closer in to the silo;
a few artful passes and they settle
for the night on its ledges and broken shingles.
As if that weren't enough to bring on darkness,
a single bird rises out of the coda:
dive, weave, dip, weave, dive, an homage.
Description is not the point.
Alone in broad arcs over pasture and dairy barn,
this fowl among fowl draws the radiance of his circling out
as far as intuition allows
and with slow steady flapping
reels it back in. The wind
is more than he remembered.
He misses warm shadows in his periphery:
without them the sky is huge, like new happiness
already faltering in a few dizzy seconds.
So he, a rock dove of the Columbidae family,
an easy mark, folds himself,
seems to float, and, like a fan
in the hands of a pastor's wife, opens
his wings, paddles the air,
and lowers himself
into the silo to roost.

Gravity

Your spidery fingers look for a wrinkle, a wound, a wraith
of gravity in the barest indentation.

Hawk-high, the coolness off the rock
comes in waves, a mineral taste.

Stack your strength like vertebrae
and balance your flight to the pull of the highway.

Be still for the rock
but for gravity, fluctuate your selves

like mercury into and out of
contiguous peninsulas of the body

to meet rock and earth sufficiently.
Read slowly with your hands, fingers, toes,

hipbones, knees, shoulders, chin
the lapidary phrasing of antagonist and helpmeet.

To the sky, Eleanor,
say, belay, belay, belay.

Dewlap

Guess how old I am.
Eyes, teeth, holes, shadow and luster,
skin pulled across small bones and muscle,
her face hurts her feelings. Loosening,
lined, spotted with mold,
the skin goes wild. Nature is time:
the Big Bang, the Do-Do Bird, and her.
How do you look so young?
One lady says, Cuban women use egg whites
and alum to pull up drooping eyelids.
Marlene Dietrich pinned back her scalp
before each scene. Three women died
this summer on Dr. Baker's table. Quietly
another says, *I don't recognize myself anymore.*
Mother's dead giveaways
you've reached a certain age: the walk,
the neck, the crepey skin between the breasts,
and talking about face lifts at dinner.

Cow

A tarp and poles pushing out at the hips,
a tent saddled with rain, she's not so much
cow anymore. What's left hangs low
off her spine like a purse, pulls her toward
the soft ground. Leaving her behind, her skin
can't help but shine like leather in the sun.

Groundhog

Eleanor said *Astonish*,
and the wind-slapped trees
brought their many hands to the sky,
then corrected themselves,
(nothing had happened)
fidgeting with the air, patting it down
into stillness again.

One spruce tossed
and roiled and popped and knew
what was coming but not when.
The tree was a conductor's hand
drawing out the storm's first tentative notes.
The air like steam from tea.
And still it did not come.

Second earth or second sky,
the fog stretched out in the pasture.
Thousands of funnel webs
as far as the eye could see
spun overnight and gemmed with dew.
Rolls of hay rotting in high wide grass.
Ayda-Lie, Ayda-Lie, Ayda-Lie.

A tendril of kudzu processes to Amherst
across the railroad bridge.
Are those bee houses or tombstones
between the hills?
She said *Astonish*. I wished
she were mine.
A groundhog on the railroad tracks.

Could it be the same groundhog
at the same juncture of rail and tie,
I'd seen the day before as I

hurtled across the bridge
through curtains of warm rain?
It's the same posture of concern:
upright in the blue midday,

spiky head held in its paws.
The moment had folded over on itself.
We were meant to meet
in this manner and then
we were reminded of it.
Despite all the fuss.
Despite all the fuss.

Eleanor

The petite bull has gotten out of the pasture.
He scrapes the gravel road and dust
puffs out of his nostrils.

All day goldfinches fall up and down,
thistle to hemlock to thistle,
their sides turn green in later light.

The formidable bullfrog has sides like a bellows.
Spiders drag around sacs of eggs while they work.
The big-eared cat kills black crickets who can't keep quiet.

Momma, momma?
Eleanor, it's time to go.

Sometimes my body is my better self.
Year after year it patiently ministers.
Half the time I'm not even trying.

Not to take this body for granted,
not to take this body down with me.
Let it be taken over

by more than it can contain. Eleanor,
I might be gone when you come back.
You might come back when I am gone.

There are too many ways to miss a life.
Eleanor, where are you?
It's time to go.

MANIFEST DESTINY

poor sparrow lights
and the branch dissolves into ash

light is the sparrow
the path is the branch

dappling light through
the batting of leaves

an afterimage of splash and spark
squeezed across the retina

light through the leaves
dissolves the path, the branch

you're suddenly up to your knees
in fern then thorn

grasping, squidlike
fastening to any soft flesh that moves

b-grade blue-gray
hand thrusts out of the loam

a crocus on speed
grabs a teen by the ankle

your time will come
when the desert slinks east

and Appalachia is a chapped lip
we will be unmanifested

unsheltered but in dinosaur time
after the trees still standing

in the Smokies after the Thanksgiving
fires have knit up their crowns

in a chlorophyll-soaked shade
oh, the dark oxygen they exhale!

words for wood that burns:
litard, fatwood, kindling, tinder

lapstrake, clinkerbuilt, clapboard, shelter
old English for shield and phalanx

we live and die so fast—
like flies to these rooted sentries

a tree has time to prepare
to burn through its sugar for a blowsy finale

before it is sapped
I hear spiders working

funnel webs in the grass
water drips from an unknown source

the tiniest bird charges the morning with song
jimmy jimmy jimmy

but the real music is the slipknot
of silence between trills

I know what inexorable feels like
the night train's layered bass and percussion

the engine's bellowy wheeze
through the round heart's ta-chunk, ta-chunk

slowly the seas rise
slowly the trees sing

in the earth's spring I will die
our children in its summer

this is not a poem of hope
but of wonder

at how dying can be
so damned beautiful

ACKNOWLEDGMENTS

Many thanks to the editors of the following journals for publishing these poems, some of them in earlier versions:

Barrow Street: "Frame" and "Hive Mind"

Birmingham Poetry Review: "Pry," "What We Might Think About . . . ," and "Promise Never"

Blackbird: "I Am Not a Man; I Am Dynamite," "Lapse," "Wild Pigs in North Georgia," and "Nebraska"

The Briar Cliff Review: "Like a Grassfire"

Catch Up: "Loneliness for Animals"

The Chattahoochee Review: "On Hollow"

Copper Nickel: "Overbite, 1969"

Fringe: "Summer Ends in Virginia"

Hopkins Review: "Jellyfish Gallery"

Interim: "Youth," "Manifest Destiny," and "Teen Hunger"

Louisville Review: "Flying Squirrel" (published as "Boomers")

Nelle: "Life Is a State of Siege . . ."

Pank: "Keel"

Pleiades: "Eggtooth"

Porter House Review: "If the Eye Were an Animal"

Salmagundi: "House of Wind"

Sidereal: "Wanting to Hold, Wanting to Fall," "Anniversary," and "The New Moon"

Stone Canoe: "The Indwelling"

StorySouth: "How to Make a Wolf"

Subtropics: "My Dream of You Isn't Over"

Tar River Poetry: "Bird in a Boat"

NOTES

From the dedication:

The quotation is from "Open City" by Teju Cole.

"If the Eye Were an Animal":

The poem's title and line "If the eye were an animal, sight would be its soul" comes from Aristotle's "On the Soul."

"Auricle":

Certain rhythms, imagery, and diction are indebted both to Richard Wilbur's poem "Love Calls Us to the Things of This World" and to Shakespeare's Sonnet 116.

"My Dream of You Isn't Over":

Thanks to Eugenio Montale's poem "The Lemons" and two translations of that poem by Millicent Bell and Jonathan Galassi.

"The Rapture" and "My Dream of You Isn't Over" make references to Luke 12:7

CPSIA information can be obtained
at www.ICGtesting.com
Printed in the USA
LVHW031136260221
680019LV00011B/248

9 781574 418248